MznLnx

Missing Links Exam Preps

Exam Prep for

Project Management : The Managerial Process

Gray & Larson, 4th Edition

The MznLnx Exam Prep is your link from the texbook and lecture to your exams.
The MznLnx Exam Preps are unauthorized and comprehensive reviews of your textbooks.

All material provided by MznLnx and Rico Publications (c) 2010
Textbook publishers and textbook authors do not particpate in or contribute to these reviews.

MznLnx

Rico
Publications

Exam Prep for Project Management : The Managerial Process
4th Edition
Gray & Larson

Publisher: Raymond Houge
Assistant Editor: Michael Rouger
Text and Cover Designer: Lisa Buckner
Marketing Manager: Sara Swagger
Project Manager, Editorial Production: Jerry Emerson
Art Director: Vernon Lowerui

Product Manager: Dave Mason
Editorial Assitant: Rachel Guzmanji
Pedagogy: Debra Long
Cover Image: Jim Reed/Getty Images
Text and Cover Printer: City Printing, Inc.
Compositor: Media Mix, Inc.

(c) 2010 Rico Publications
ALL RIGHTS RESERVED. No part of this work covered by the copyright may be reproduced or used in any form or by an means--graphic, electronic, or mechanical, including photocopying, recording, taping, Web distribution, information storage, and retrieval systems, or in any other manner--without the written permission of the publisher.

Printed in the United States
ISBN:

For more information about our products, contact us at:
Dave.Mason@RicoPublications.com

For permission to use material from this text or product, submit a request online to:
Dave.Mason@RicoPublications.com

Contents

CHAPTER 1
Modern Project Management   1

CHAPTER 2
Organization Strategy and Project Selection   6

CHAPTER 3
Organization: Structure and Culture   14

CHAPTER 4
Defining the Project   16

CHAPTER 5
Estimating Project Times and Costs   19

CHAPTER 6
Developing a Project Plan   23

CHAPTER 7
Managing Risk   26

CHAPTER 8
Scheduling Resources and Costs   30

CHAPTER 9
Reducing Project Duration   33

CHAPTER 10
Leadership: Being an Effective Project Manager   37

CHAPTER 11
Managing Project Teams   42

CHAPTER 12
Outsourcing: Managing Interorganizational Relations   47

CHAPTER 13
Progress and Performance Measurement and Evaluation   51

CHAPTER 14
Project Audit and Closure   55

CHAPTER 15
International Projects   56

CHAPTER 16
Oversight   58

ANSWER KEY   60

TO THE STUDENT

COMPREHENSIVE

The *MznLnx* Exam Prep series is designed to help you pass your exams. Editors at MznLnx review your textbooks and then prepare these practice exams to help you master the textbook material. Unlike study guides, workbooks, and practice tests provided by the texbook publisher and textbook authors, *MznLnx* gives you **all** of the material in each chapter in exam form, not just samples, so you can be sure to nail your exam.

MECHANICAL

The MznLnx Exam Prep series creates exams that will help you learn the subject matter as well as test you on your understanding. Each question is designed to help you master the concept. Just working through the exams, you gain an understanding of the subject--its a simple mechanical process that produces success.

INTEGRATED STUDY GUIDE AND REVIEW

MznLnx is not just a set of exams designed to test you, its also a comprehensive review of the subject content. Each exam question is also a review of the concept, making sure that you will get the answer correct without having to go to other sources of material. You learn as you go! Its the easiest way to pass an exam.

HUMOR

Studying can be tedious and dry. MznLnx's instructional design includes moderate humor within the exam questions on occassion, to break the tedium and revitalize the brain

Chapter 1. Modern Project Management   1

1. _____ is the discipline of planning, organizing and managing resources to bring about the successful completion of specific project goals and objectives.

A project is a finite endeavor--having specific start and completion dates--undertaken to meet particular goals and objectives, usually to bring about beneficial change or added value. This finite characteristic of projects stands in contrast to processes, or operations--which is repetitive, permanent or semi-permanent functional work to produce products or services.

   a. Project Management
   b. Risk register
   c. SMART
   d. Logical framework approach

2. _____ , as defined by the _____ Association of America (Information technologyAA), is 'the study, design, development, implementation, support or management of computer-based information systems, particularly software applications and computer hardware.' _____ deals with the use of electronic computers and computer software to convert, store, protect, process, transmit, and securely retrieve information.

Today, the term _____ has ballooned to encompass many aspects of computing and technology, and the term has become very recognizable. The _____ umbrella can be quite large, covering many fields.

   a. Information technology
   b. AACE International
   c. AACR2
   d. ACID

3. _____ is a credential offered by the Project Management Institute (PMI.) The credential is obtained by documenting your work experience in project management, completing 35 hours of project management related training, and scoring at least 61% on a written, multiple choice examination. _____ exams administered on or before June 30, 2009 will be based on 'A Guide to the Project Management Body of Knowledge - or PMBOK,' the Third Edition.
   a. Back-end database
   b. 8.3 filename
   c. Project Management Professional
   d. 68-95-99.7 rule

4. A _____ is a professional in the field of project management. _____s can have the responsibility of the planning, execution, and closing of any project, typically relating to construction industry, architecture, computer networking, telecommunications or software development.

Many other fields in the production, design and service industries also have _____s.

a. Schedule chicken
b. Logical framework approach
c. Project management office
d. Project manager

5. _____ in organizations and public policy is both the organizational process of creating and maintaining a plan; and the psychological process of thinking about the activities required to create a desired goal on some scale. As such, it is a fundamental property of intelligent behavior. This thought process is essential to the creation and refinement of a plan, or integration of it with other plans, that is, it combines forecasting of developments with the preparation of scenarios of how to react to them.
a. Planning
b. 8.3 filename
c. 68-95-99.7 rule
d. Back-end database

6. A _____ in project management and systems engineering, is a tool used to define and group a project's discrete work elements (or tasks) in a way that helps organize and define the total work scope of the project.

A _____ element may be a product, data, a service, or any combination. A _____ also provides the necessary framework for detailed cost estimating and control along with providing guidance for schedule development and control.

a. 68-95-99.7 rule
b. Work breakdown structure
c. Back-end database
d. 8.3 filename

7.

_____ is, in very basic words, a position a firm occupies against its competitors.

According to Michael Porter, the three methods for creating a sustainable _____ are through:

1. Cost leadership - Cost advantage occurs when a firm delivers the same services as its competitors but at a lower cost;

2. Differentiation - Differentiation advantage occurs when a firm delivers greater services for the same price of its competitors. They are collectively known as positional advantages because they denote the firm's position in its industry as a leader in either superior services or cost;

3. Focus (economics) - A focused approach requires the firm to concentrate on a narrow, exclusive competitive segment (market niche), hoping to achieve a local rather than industry wide _____.

a. 68-95-99.7 rule
b. Competitive advantage
c. Back-end database
d. 8.3 filename

8. _____ is a family of standards for quality management systems. _____ is maintained by ISO, the International Organization for Standardization and is administered by accreditation and certification bodies. The rules are updated, the time and changes in the requirements for quality, motivate change.

a. ISO 9000
b. AACE International
c. ACID
d. AACR2

9. _____ Management is the succession of strategies used by management as a product goes through its _____. The conditions in which a product is sold changes over time and must be managed as it moves through its succession of stages.

The _____ goes through many phases, involves many professional disciplines, and requires many skills, tools and processes.

a. Knowledge spillover
b. Business Technology Management
c. Customer satisfaction
d. Product life cycle

10. In commerce, _____ is the length of time it takes from a product being conceived until its being available for sale. _____ is important in industries where products are outmoded quickly. A common assumption is that _____ matters most for first-of-a-kind products, but actually the leader often has the luxury of time, while the clock is clearly running for the followers.

a. Service Network
b. Product life cycle
c. Sensitivity analysis
d. Time to market

11. _____, a business term, is a measure of how products and services supplied by a company meet or surpass customer expectation. It is seen as a key performance indicator within business and is part of the four perspectives of a Balanced Scorecard.

In a competitive marketplace where businesses compete for customers, _____ is seen as a key differentiator and increasingly has become a key element of business strategy.

   a. Business Technology Management
   b. Sensitivity analysis
   c. Time to market
   d. Customer satisfaction

12. _____ is an organization's process of defining its strategy and making decisions on allocating its resources to pursue this strategy, including its capital and people. Various business analysis techniques can be used in _____, including SWOT analysis (Strengths, Weaknesses, Opportunities, and Threats) and PEST analysis (Political, Economic, Social, and Technological analysis) or STEER analysis (Socio-cultural, Technological, Economic, Ecological, and Regulatory factors) and EPISTEL (Environment, Political, Informatic, Social, Technological, Economic and Legal)

_____ is the formal consideration of an organization's future course. All _____ deals with at least one of three key questions:

   1. 'What do we do?'
   2. 'For whom do we do it?'
   3. 'How do we excel?'

In business _____, the third question is better phrased 'How can we beat or avoid competition?'. (Bradford and Duncan, page 1.)

   a. Back-end database
   b. 68-95-99.7 rule
   c. 8.3 filename
   d. Strategic planning

13. _____ is a process of planning and controlling the performance or execution of any type of activity, such as:

   - a project (project _____) or
   - a process (process _____, sometimes referred to as the process performance measurement and management system.)

Organization's senior management is responsible for carrying out its _____.

a. Back-end database
b. 68-95-99.7 rule
c. 8.3 filename
d. Management process

14. A _____ is the management process of planning and controlling the performance or execution of a project.

- Documented need to act
- Project plan templates
- Lessons learned from previous projects
- Existing project management standards
- External information
- Resources for project planning and project execution

- Project initiation
- Project planning
- Project execution
- Project control and validation
- Project closeout and evaluation

- Project products delivered
- Project objectives achieved (as a result of the interplay among project products and the organization or its environment)
- Lessons learned documented

a. Product breakdown structure
b. Resource Breakdown Structure
c. Project cancellation
d. Project management process

Chapter 2. Organization Strategy and Project Selection

1. Models of the _____ effect and the closely related experience curve effect express the relationship between equations for experience and efficiency or between efficiency gains and investment in the effort. The experience of '_____s' was first observed by the 19th Century German psychologist Hermann Ebbinghaus according to the difficulty of memorizing varying numbers of verbal stimuli, and subsequent learning about the complex processes of learning are discussed in the

   .

   The rule used for representing the _____ effect states that the more times a task has been performed, the less time will be required on each subsequent iteration.

   a. 68-95-99.7 rule
   b. 8.3 filename
   c. Learning curve
   d. Back-end database

2. _____ is a process of planning and controlling the performance or execution of any type of activity, such as:

   - a project (project _____) or
   - a process (process _____, sometimes referred to as the process performance measurement and management system.)

   Organization's senior management is responsible for carrying out its _____.

   a. Management process
   b. Back-end database
   c. 68-95-99.7 rule
   d. 8.3 filename

3. _____ is a process of gathering, analyzing, and dispensing information for tactical or strategic purposes. The _____ process entails obtaining both factual and subjective information on the business environments in which a company is operating or considering entering.

   There are three ways of scanning the business environment:

   - Ad-hoc scanning - Short term, infrequent examinations usually initiated by a crisis
   - Regular scanning - Studies done on a regular schedule (say, once a year)
   - Continuous scanning(also called continuous learning) - continuous structured data collection and processing on a broad range of environmental factors

   Most commentators feel that in today's turbulent business environment the best scanning method available is continuous scanning.This allows the firm to :

-act quickly-take advantage of opportunities before competitors do-respond to environmental threats before significant damage is done

The Macro Environment

_____ usually refers just to the macro environment, but it can also include:-industry -competitor analysis -marketing research(consumer analysis) -New Product Development(product innovations)- the company's internal environment

Macro _____ involves analysing:

- The Economy

GDP per capitaeconomic growthunemployment]] rateinflation]] rateconsumer and investor confidenceinventory levelscurrency exchange ratesmerchandise trade balancefinancial and political health of trading partnersbalance of paymentsfuture trends

- Government

political climate - amount of government activitypolitical stability and riskgovernment debtbudget deficit or surpluscorporate and personal tax ratespayroll taxesimport tariffs and quotasexport restrictionsrestrictions on international financial flows

- Legal

minimum wage lawsenvironmental protection lawsworker safety lawsunion lawscopyright and patent lawsanti- monopoly lawsSunday closing lawsmunicipal licenceslaws that favour business investment

- Technology

efficiency of infrastructure, including: roads, ports, airports, rolling stock, hospitals, education, healthcare, communication, etc.industrial productivitynew manufacturing processesnew products and services of competitorsnew products and services of supply chain partnersany new technology that could impact the companycost and accessibility of electrical power

- Ecology
    - ecological concerns that affect the firms production processes
    - ecological concerns that affect customers' buying habits
    - ecological concerns that affect customers' perception of the company or product
- Socio-Cultural
    - demographic factors such as:
        - population size and distribution
        - age distribution
        - education levels
        - income levels
        - ethnic origins
        - religious affiliations
    - attitudes towards:
        - materialism, capitalism, free enterprise
        - individualism, role of family, role of government, collectivism
        - role of church and religion
        - consumerism
        - environmentalism
        - importance of work, pride of accomplishment
    - cultural structures including:
        - diet and nutrition
        - housing conditions
- Potential Suppliers
    - Labour supply
        - quantity of labour available
        - quality of labour available
        - stability of labour supply
        - wage expectations
        - employee turn-over rate
        - strikes and labour relations
        - educational facilities
    - Material suppliers
        - quality, quantity, price, and stability of material inputs
        - delivery delays
        - proximity of bulky or heavy material inputs
        - level of competition among suppliers
    - Service Providers
        - quantity, quality, price, and stability of service facilitators
        - special requirements
- Stakeholders
    - Lobbyists
    - Shareholders
    - Employees
    - Partners

Scanning these macro environmental variables for threats and opportunities requires that each issue be rated on two dimensions. It must be rated on its potential impact on the company, and rated on its likeliness of occurrence.

a. Environmental scanning
b. AACE International
c. ACID
d. AACR2

4. _____ is the process of comparing the cost, cycle time, productivity, or quality of a specific process or method to another that is widely considered to be an industry standard or best practice. Essentially, _____ provides a snapshot of the performance of your business and helps you understand where you are in relation to a particular standard. The result is often a business case for making changes in order to make improvements.

a. 8.3 filename
b. Back-end database
c. Benchmarking
d. 68-95-99.7 rule

5. _____ is a strategic planning method used to evaluate the Strengths, Weaknesses, Opportunities, and Threats involved in a project or in a business venture. It involves specifying the objective of the business venture or project and identifying the internal and external factors that are favorable and unfavorable to achieving that objective. The technique is credited to Albert Humphrey, who led a convention at Stanford University in the 1960s and 1970s using data from Fortune 500 companies.

a. Customer relationship management
b. SWOT analysis
c. 68-95-99.7 rule
d. Customer to customer

6. _____ is a term used by project managers and project management (PM) organizations to describe methods for analyzing and collectively managing a group of current or proposed projects based on numerous key characteristics. The fundamental objective of the _____ process is to determine the optimal mix and sequencing of proposed projects to best achieve the organization's overall goals - typically expressed in terms of hard economic measures, business strategy goals, or technical strategy goals - while honoring constraints imposed by management or external real-world factors. Typical attributes of projects being analyzed in a _____ process include each project's total expected cost, consumption of scarce resources (human or otherwise) expected timeline and schedule of investment, expected nature, magnitude and timing of benefits to be realized, and relationship or inter-dependencies with other projects in the portfolio.

a. Document Imaging
b. Customer intelligence
c. Records management
d. Project portfolio management

7. _____ Programme and Project Management Maturity Model is a reference guide for structured best practice. It breaks down the broad disciplines of portfolio, programme and project management into a hierarchy of Key Process Areas The hierarchical approach enables organisations to assess their current capability and then plot a roadmap for improvement prioritised by those KPAs which will make the biggest impact on performance.
a. 8.3 filename
b. Back-end database
c. 68-95-99.7 rule
d. P3M3

8. In computing, a _____ or network share is a device or piece of information on a computer that can be remotely accessed from another computer, typically via a local area network or an enterprise Intranet, as if it were a resource in the local machine.

Examples are shared file access (also known as disk sharing and folder sharing), shared printer access (printer sharing), shared scanner access, etc. The _____ is called a shared disk (also known as mounted disk), shared drive volume, shared folder, shared file, shared document, shared printer or shared scanner.

a. Back-end database
b. 68-95-99.7 rule
c. Shared resource
d. 8.3 filename

9. _____ or net present worth (NPW) is defined as the total present value (PV) of a time series of cash flows. It is a standard method for using the time value of money to appraise long-term projects. Used for capital budgeting, and widely throughout economics, it measures the excess or shortfall of cash flows, in present value terms, once financing charges are met.
a. Back-end database
b. 8.3 filename
c. 68-95-99.7 rule
d. Net present value

10. A core competency is a specific factor that a business sees as being central to the way it, or its employees work. It fulfils three key criteria:

1. It provides consumer benefits
2. It is not easy for competitors to imitate
3. It can be leveraged widely to many products and markets.

A core competency can take various forms, including technical/subject matter know-how, a reliable process and/or close relationships with customers and suppliers. It may also include product development or culture, such as employee dedication.

_____ are particular strengths relative to other organizations in the industry which provide the fundamental basis for the provision of added value.

a. 68-95-99.7 rule
b. Core competencies
c. Back-end database
d. 8.3 filename

11. The _____ is an interest rate a central bank charges depository institutions that borrow reserves from it.

The term _____ has two meanings:

- the same as interest rate; the term 'discount' does not refer to the meaning of the word, but to the purpose of using the quantity, such as computations of present value, e.g. net present value or discounted cash flow

- the annual effective _____, which is the annual interest divided by the capital including that interest; this rate is lower than the interest rate; it corresponds to using the value after a year as the nominal value, and seeing the initial value as the nominal value minus a discount; it is used for Treasury Bills and similar financial instruments

The annual effective _____ is the annual interest divided by the capital including that interest, which is the interest rate divided by 100% plus the interest rate. It is the annual discount factor to be applied to the future cash flow, to find the discount, subtracted from a future value to find the value one year earlier.

For example, suppose there is a government bond that sells for $95 and pays $100 in a year's time.

a. Discount rate
b. 8.3 filename
c. Back-end database
d. 68-95-99.7 rule

Chapter 2. Organization Strategy and Project Selection

12. A request for proposal (referred to as _____) is an invitation for suppliers, often through a bidding process, to submit a proposal on a specific commodity or service. A bidding process is one of the best methods for leveraging a company's negotiating ability and purchasing power with suppliers. The _____ process brings structure to the procurement decision and allows the risks and benefits to be identified clearly upfront.

   a. 8.3 filename
   b. RFP
   c. 68-95-99.7 rule
   d. Back-end database

13. A _____ is a valuable possession of which its owner cannot dispose and whose cost (particularly cost of upkeep) is out of proportion to its usefulness.

The term derives from the sacred _____s kept by Southeast Asian monarchs in Burma, Thailand, Laos and Cambodia. To possess a _____ was regarded (and is still regarded in Thailand and Burma) as a sign that the monarch was ruling with justice and power, and that the kingdom was blessed with peace and prosperity.

   a. 68-95-99.7 rule
   b. 8.3 filename
   c. Back-end database
   d. White elephant

14. A _____ is a group or individual that contracts with another organization or individual (the owner) for the construction, renovation or demolition of a building, road or other structure. A _____ is defined as such if it is the signatory as the builder of the prime construction contract for the project.

A _____ is responsible for the means and methods to be used in the construction execution of the project in accordance with the contract documents.

   a. 68-95-99.7 rule
   b. 8.3 filename
   c. General contractor
   d. Back-end database

15. A _____ is a document that captures and agrees the work activities, deliverables and timeline that a vendor will execute against in performance of work for a customer. Detailed requirements and pricing are usually specified in a _____, along with many other terms and conditions.

There are many formats and styles of _____ document templates that have been specialized for the Hardware or Software solutions being described in the Request for Proposal.

a. Statement of work
b. 8.3 filename
c. Back-end database
d. 68-95-99.7 rule

Chapter 3. Organization: Structure and Culture

1. _____ is the discipline of planning, organizing and managing resources to bring about the successful completion of specific project goals and objectives.

A project is a finite endeavor--having specific start and completion dates--undertaken to meet particular goals and objectives, usually to bring about beneficial change or added value. This finite characteristic of projects stands in contrast to processes, or operations--which is repetitive, permanent or semi-permanent functional work to produce products or services.

   a. SMART
   b. Logical framework approach
   c. Risk register
   d. Project management

2. A _____ is a team whose members usually belong to different groups, functions and are assigned to activities for the same project. A team can be divided into sub-teams according to need. Usually _____s are only used for a defined period of time.
   a. Project manager
   b. Project management 2.0
   c. Certified project manager
   d. Project team

3. _____ is a type of organizational management in which people with similar skills are pooled for work assignments. For example, all engineers may be in one engineering department and report to an engineering manager, but these same engineers may be assigned to different projects and report to a project manager while working on that project. Therefore, each engineer may have to work under several managers to get their job done.
   a. Workflow Management Coalition
   b. Matrix Management
   c. Micromanagement
   d. Managing stage boundaries

4. A _____ in project management and systems engineering, is a tool used to define and group a project's discrete work elements (or tasks) in a way that helps organize and define the total work scope of the project.

A _____ element may be a product, data, a service, or any combination. A _____ also provides the necessary framework for detailed cost estimating and control along with providing guidance for schedule development and control.

a. Back-end database
b. Work breakdown structure
c. 8.3 filename
d. 68-95-99.7 rule

Chapter 4. Defining the Project

1. _____ in project management is a tangible or intangible object produced as a result of project execution, as part of an obligation. The term can be either a noun: an item, product or artifact which must be created and then delivered as part of an obligation, or an adjective: describing something which must be delivered as part of an obligation. Like many terms common in corporate usage, the word is considered corporate jargon or corporatese, referring specifically to goals.
   a. Negative volume index
   b. Pivot point calculations
   c. 68-95-99.7 rule
   d. Deliverable

2. In project management, a _____ or project definition (sometimes called the terms of reference) is a statement of the scope, objectives and participants in a project. It provides a preliminary delineation of roles and responsibilities, outlines the project objectives, identifies the main stakeholders, and defines the authority of the project manager. It serves as a reference of authority for the future of the project.
   a. SimulTrain
   b. Cone of Uncertainty
   c. Project management plan
   d. Project charter

3. A _____ is a document that captures and agrees the work activities, deliverables and timeline that a vendor will execute against in performance of work for a customer. Detailed requirements and pricing are usually specified in a _____, along with many other terms and conditions.

   There are many formats and styles of _____ document templates that have been specialized for the Hardware or Software solutions being described in the Request for Proposal.

   a. Back-end database
   b. 8.3 filename
   c. 68-95-99.7 rule
   d. Statement of work

4. _____s may take many forms depending on the type of project being implemented and the nature of the organization. The _____ details the project deliverables and describes the major objectives. The objectives should include measurable success criteria for the project.
   a. Stealth mode
   b. Project initiation document
   c. Timeboxing
   d. Scope statement

Chapter 4. Defining the Project

5. _____ in project management refers to uncontrolled changes in a project's scope. This phenomenon can occur when the scope of a project is not properly defined, documented, or controlled. It is generally considered a negative occurrence that is to be avoided.
   a. Scope creep
   b. Student syndrome
   c. Graphical Evaluation and Review Technique
   d. Problem domain analysis

6. A _____ is an explicit set of requirements to be satisfied by a material, product, or service. Should a material, product or service fail to meet one or more of the applicable _____s, it may be referred to as being out of specificiation; the abbreviation OOS may also be used.

A technical _____ may be developed privately, for example by a corporation, regulatory body, military, etc.

   a. 68-95-99.7 rule
   b. 8.3 filename
   c. Specification
   d. Back-end database

7. A _____ in project management and systems engineering, is a tool used to define and group a project's discrete work elements (or tasks) in a way that helps organize and define the total work scope of the project.

A _____ element may be a product, data, a service, or any combination. A _____ also provides the necessary framework for detailed cost estimating and control along with providing guidance for schedule development and control.

   a. Work breakdown structure
   b. 68-95-99.7 rule
   c. Back-end database
   d. 8.3 filename

8. In project management, a _____ is a subset of a project that can be assigned to a specific party for execution. Because of the similarity, _____s are often misidentified as projects.

Similar to a work breakdown structure, a _____ is part of a Plan Breakdown Structure, representing a collection of work actions necessary to create a specific result.

a. Risk register
b. Precedence Diagram Method
c. Work package
d. Constructability

9. In a general sense, the term _____ refers to a system of people, data records and activities that process the data and information in an organization, and it includes the organization's manual and automated processes. In a narrow sense, the term _____ refers to the specific application software that is used to store data records in a computer system and automates some of the information-processing activities of the organization. Computer-based _____s are in the field of information technology.
   a. AACE International
   b. AACR2
   c. ACID
   d. Information system

10. _____ is a term used in project management and business administration to describe a process where all the individuals or groups that are likely to be affected by the activities of a project are identified and then sorted according to how much they can affect the project and how much the project can affect them. This information is used to assess how the interests of those stakeholders should be addressed in the project plan.

A stakeholder is any person or organization, who can be positively or negatively impacted by, or cause an impact on the actions of a company.

   a. 68-95-99.7 rule
   b. 8.3 filename
   c. Back-end database
   d. Stakeholder analysis

Chapter 5. Estimating Project Times and Costs

1. _____ in organizations and public policy is both the organizational process of creating and maintaining a plan; and the psychological process of thinking about the activities required to create a desired goal on some scale. As such, it is a fundamental property of intelligent behavior. This thought process is essential to the creation and refinement of a plan, or integration of it with other plans, that is, it combines forecasting of developments with the preparation of scenarios of how to react to them.
   a. Back-end database
   b. 68-95-99.7 rule
   c. 8.3 filename
   d. Planning

2. A _____ is a fixed point of time in the future at which point certain processes will be evaluated or assumed to end. It is necessary in an accounting, finance or risk management regime to assign such a fixed horizon time so that alternatives can be evaluated for performance over the same period of time. A _____ is a physical impossibility in the real world.
   a. Project management office
   b. Time horizon
   c. Project management 2.0
   d. Mandated Lead Arranger

3. A _____ in project management and systems engineering, is a tool used to define and group a project's discrete work elements (or tasks) in a way that helps organize and define the total work scope of the project.

   A _____ element may be a product, data, a service, or any combination. A _____ also provides the necessary framework for detailed cost estimating and control along with providing guidance for schedule development and control.

   a. 68-95-99.7 rule
   b. Back-end database
   c. Work breakdown structure
   d. 8.3 filename

4. _____ are a restriction on philosophical arguments, especially in epistemology, in order to avoid objections perceived as digressive. As a reply to objections to an explanation of a phenomenon, e.g. a hypothesis or a theory, it is said, argument X holds [only] under _____. In some cases, the concept of _____ tends to be rather blurred and the reply under _____ can tend to extend to everything that contradicts an argument.
   a. 68-95-99.7 rule
   b. Back-end database
   c. 8.3 filename
   d. Normal conditions

5. In project management, a _____ is a subset of a project that can be assigned to a specific party for execution. Because of the similarity, _____s are often misidentified as projects.

Similar to a work breakdown structure, a _____ is part of a Plan Breakdown Structure, representing a collection of work actions necessary to create a specific result.

   a. Risk register
   b. Work package
   c. Constructability
   d. Precedence Diagram Method

6. _____ in the English language is defined firstly as unanimous or general agreement; and secondly group solidarity of belief or sentiment.

Idyllically, achieving _____ requires serious treatment of every group member's considered opinion. Those who wish to take up some action want to hear those who oppose it, because they count on the fact that the ensuing debate will improve the _____.

   a. Back-end database
   b. 8.3 filename
   c. 68-95-99.7 rule
   d. Consensus

7. The _____ is a systematic, interactive forecasting method which relies on a panel of independent experts. The carefully selected experts answer questionnaires in two or more rounds. After each round, a facilitator provides an anonymous summary of the experts' forecasts from the previous round as well as the reasons they provided for their judgments.
   a. Learning organization
   b. Group decision support systems
   c. Service innovation
   d. Delphi method

8. The _____ refers to a cognitive bias whereby the perception of a particular trait is influenced by the perception of the former traits in a sequence of interpretations.

Edward L. Thorndike was the first to support the _____ with empirical research. In a psychology study published in 1920, Thorndike asked commanding officers to rate their soldiers; Thorndike found high cross-correlation between all positive and all negative traits.

a. 68-95-99.7 rule
b. 8.3 filename
c. Halo effect
d. Back-end database

9. Models of the _____ effect and the closely related experience curve effect express the relationship between equations for experience and efficiency or between efficiency gains and investment in the effort. The experience of '_____s' was first observed by the 19th Century German psychologist Hermann Ebbinghaus according to the difficulty of memorizing varying numbers of verbal stimuli, and subsequent learning about the complex processes of learning are discussed in the

.

The rule used for representing the _____ effect states that the more times a task has been performed, the less time will be required on each subsequent iteration.

a. 8.3 filename
b. 68-95-99.7 rule
c. Back-end database
d. Learning curve

10. In a general sense, the term _____ refers to a system of people, data records and activities that process the data and information in an organization, and it includes the organization's manual and automated processes. In a narrow sense, the term _____ refers to the specific application software that is used to store data records in a computer system and automates some of the information-processing activities of the organization. Computer-based _____s are in the field of information technology.
a. AACE International
b. ACID
c. AACR2
d. Information system

11. _____s are expenses that change in proportion to the activity of a business. In other words, _____ is the sum of marginal costs. It can also be considered normal costs.
a. Back-end database
b. 8.3 filename
c. Variable cost
d. 68-95-99.7 rule

Chapter 5. Estimating Project Times and Costs

12. A _____ is a structured collection of records or data that is stored in a computer system. The structure is achieved by organizing the data according to a _____ model. The model that is most commonly used today is the relational model.
   a. 8.3 filename
   b. Back-end database
   c. 68-95-99.7 rule
   d. Database

13. Models of the learning curve effect and the closely related _____ effect express the relationship between equations for experience and efficiency or between efficiency gains and investment in the effort. The experience of 'learning curves' was first observed by the 19th Century German psychologist Hermann Ebbinghaus according to the difficulty of memorizing varying numbers of verbal stimuli, and subsequent learning about the complex processes of learning are discussed in the

The rule used for representing the learning curve effect states that the more times a task has been performed, the less time will be required on each subsequent iteration.

   a. AACE International
   b. AACR2
   c. ACID
   d. Experience curve

Chapter 6. Developing a Project Plan

1. A _____ is a graph (flow chart) depicting the sequence in which a project's terminal elements are to be completed by showing terminal elements and their dependencies.

The work breakdown structure or the product breakdown structure show the 'part-whole' relations. In contrast, the _____ shows the 'before-after' relations.

   a. Project network
   b. Back-end database
   c. 68-95-99.7 rule
   d. 8.3 filename

2. In project management, a _____ is a subset of a project that can be assigned to a specific party for execution. Because of the similarity, _____s are often misidentified as projects.

Similar to a work breakdown structure, a _____ is part of a Plan Breakdown Structure, representing a collection of work actions necessary to create a specific result.

   a. Precedence Diagram Method
   b. Constructability
   c. Risk register
   d. Work package

3. The _____ is a tool for scheduling activities in a project plan. It is a method of constructing a project schedule network diagram that uses boxes, referred to as nodes, to represent activities and connects them with arrows that show the dependencies.

   - Critical Tasks, noncritical tasks, and slack time
   - Shows the relationship of the tasks to each other
   - Allows for what-if, worst-case, best-case and most likely scenario

Key elements include determining predecessors and defining attributes such as

   - early start date
   - last-last
   - early finish date
   - late finish date
   - Duration
   - WBS reference

Chapter 6. Developing a Project Plan

   a. Kick-off Meeting
   b. Product based planning
   c. Technology roadmap
   d. Precedence diagram method

4. The _____, abbreviated _____ is a mathematically based algorithm for scheduling a set of project activities. It is an important tool for effective project management.

It was developed in the 1950s by the Dupont Corporation at about the same time that General Dynamics and the US Navy were developing the Program Evaluation and Review Technique (PERT) Today, it is commonly used with all forms of projects, including construction, software development, research projects, product development, engineering, and plant maintenance, among others.

   a. 8.3 filename
   b. Critical path method
   c. Back-end database
   d. 68-95-99.7 rule

5. A _____ is a type of bar chart that illustrates a project schedule. _____s illustrate the start and finish dates of the terminal elements and summary elements of a project. Terminal elements and summary elements comprise the work breakdown structure of the project.
   a. 68-95-99.7 rule
   b. Back-end database
   c. Gantt chart
   d. 8.3 filename

6. _____ is an investment technique that requires investors to purchase multiple financial products with different maturity dates.

_____ avoids the risk of reinvesting a big portion of assets in an unfavorable financial environment. For example, a person has both a 2015 matured CD and a 2018 matured CD.

   a. 68-95-99.7 rule
   b. Laddering
   c. Back-end database
   d. 8.3 filename

Chapter 6. Developing a Project Plan

7. _____ is a work methodology based on the parallelization of tasks (ie. concurrently.) It refers to an approach used in product development in which functions of design engineering, manufacturing engineering and other functions are integrated to reduce the elapsed time required to bring a new product to the market.
   a. Product description
   b. Project Management Simulator
   c. Cone of Uncertainty
   d. Concurrent engineering

8. A _____ or datacenter is a facility used to house computer systems and associated components, such as telecommunications and storage systems. It generally includes redundant or backup power supplies, redundant data communications connections, environmental controls and security devices.

   _____s have their roots in the huge computer rooms of the early ages of the computing industry.

   a. Microsoft Query by Example
   b. Database server
   c. Data Center
   d. Data quality assurance

Chapter 7. Managing Risk

1. _____ is the identification, assessment, and prioritization of risks followed by coordinated and economical application of resources to minimize, monitor, and control the probability and/or impact of unfortunate events.. Risks can come from uncertainty in financial markets, project failures, legal liabilities, credit risk, accidents, natural causes and disasters as well as deliberate attacks from an adversary. Several _____ standards have been developed including the Project Management Institute, the National Institute of Science and Technology, actuarial societies, and ISO standards.
    a. Signals intelligence
    b. Risk management
    c. Regression toward the mean
    d. Stitch Pipeline

2. _____ is a group creativity technique designed to generate a large number of ideas for the solution of a problem. The method was first popularized in the late 1930s by Alex Faickney Osborn in a book called Applied Imagination. Osborn proposed that groups could double their creative output with _____.
    a. Brainstorming
    b. Solutions Architect
    c. Item tree analysis
    d. Anthony Judge

3. _____ - A hierarchically organised depiction of the identified project risks arranged by category.

In Project Management, the Risk Management Process has the objectives of identifying, assessing, and managing risks, both positive and negative. All too often, project managers focus only on negative risk, however, good things can happen in a project, 'things' that were foreseen, but not really planned for.

    a. Risk breakdown structure
    b. 68-95-99.7 rule
    c. 8.3 filename
    d. Scenario analysis

4. The general definition of an _____ is an evaluation of a person, organization, system, process, project or product. _____s are performed to ascertain the validity and reliability of information; also to provide an assessment of a system's internal control. The goal of an _____ is to express an opinion on the person / organization/system (etc) in question, under evaluation based on work done on a test basis.
    a. AACE International
    b. ACID
    c. AACR2
    d. Audit

Chapter 7. Managing Risk

5. A _____ is a team whose members usually belong to different groups, functions and are assigned to activities for the same project. A team can be divided into sub-teams according to need. Usually _____s are only used for a defined period of time.
   a. Project management 2.0
   b. Project team
   c. Certified project manager
   d. Project manager

6. _____ is a term used to describe a process of preparing and collecting data - for example as part of a process improvement or similar project. The purpose of _____ is to obtain information to keep on record, to make decisions about important issues, to pass information on to others. Primarily, data is collected to provide information regarding a specific topic .
   a. Test method
   b. Data collection
   c. Public survey
   d. General Social Survey

7. _____ is a process of analyzing possible future events by considering alternative possible outcomes (scenarios.)

The analysis is designed to allow improved decision-making by allowing consideration of outcomes and their implications.

_____ can also be used to illuminate 'wild cards.' For example, analysis of the possibility of the earth being struck by a large celestial object (a meteor) suggests that whilst the probability is low, the damage inflicted is so high that the event is much more important (threatening) than the low probability (in any one year) alone would suggest.

   a. 68-95-99.7 rule
   b. Scenario analysis
   c. Systems thinking
   d. 8.3 filename

8. A _____ is a decision support tool that uses a tree-like graph or model of decisions and their possible consequences, including chance event outcomes, resource costs, and utility. _____s are commonly used in operations research, specifically in decision analysis, to help identify a strategy most likely to reach a goal. Another use of _____s is as a descriptive means for calculating conditional probabilities.

a. 68-95-99.7 rule
b. 8.3 filename
c. Back-end database
d. Decision tree

9. A _____ (FMEA) is a procedure for analysis of potential failure modes within a system for classification by severity or determination of the effect of failures on the system. It is widely used in manufacturing industries in various phases of the product life cycle and is now increasingly finding use in the service industry. Failure modes are any errors or defects in a process, design, or item, especially those that affect the customer, and can be potential or actual.
   a. Back-end database
   b. 8.3 filename
   c. Failure modes and effects analysis
   d. 68-95-99.7 rule

10. _____ or net present worth (NPW) is defined as the total present value (PV) of a time series of cash flows. It is a standard method for using the time value of money to appraise long-term projects. Used for capital budgeting, and widely throughout economics, it measures the excess or shortfall of cash flows, in present value terms, once financing charges are met.
    a. Back-end database
    b. 68-95-99.7 rule
    c. 8.3 filename
    d. Net present value

11. A _____ is an initiating cause of a causal chain which leads to an outcome or effect of interest. Commonly, _____ is used to describe the depth in the causal chain where an intervention could reasonably be implemented to change performance and prevent an undesirable outcome.

The term _____ has been used in professional journals as early as 1905, but the lack of a widely accepted definition after all this time indicates that there are significantly different interpretations of exactly what constitutes a _____.

   a. 8.3 filename
   b. Back-end database
   c. 68-95-99.7 rule
   d. Root cause

12. _____ in organizations and public policy is both the organizational process of creating and maintaining a plan; and the psychological process of thinking about the activities required to create a desired goal on some scale. As such, it is a fundamental property of intelligent behavior. This thought process is essential to the creation and refinement of a plan, or integration of it with other plans, that is, it combines forecasting of developments with the preparation of scenarios of how to react to them.

   a. Back-end database
   b. 8.3 filename
   c. 68-95-99.7 rule
   d. Planning

13. The _____, abbreviated _____ is a mathematically based algorithm for scheduling a set of project activities. It is an important tool for effective project management.

It was developed in the 1950s by the Dupont Corporation at about the same time that General Dynamics and the US Navy were developing the Program Evaluation and Review Technique (PERT) Today, it is commonly used with all forms of projects, including construction, software development, research projects, product development, engineering, and plant maintenance, among others.

   a. 8.3 filename
   b. 68-95-99.7 rule
   c. Back-end database
   d. Critical path method

14. In probability theory and statistics, the _____ or Gaussian distribution is a continuous probability distribution that describes data that clusters around a mean or average. The graph of the associated probability density function is bell-shaped, with a peak at the mean, and is known as the Gaussian function or bell curve.

The _____ can be used to describe, at least approximately, any variable that tends to cluster around the mean.

   a. Regression discontinuity
   b. First-hitting-time models
   c. Test set
   d. Normal distribution

Chapter 8. Scheduling Resources and Costs

1. In statistics and image processing, to smooth a data set is to create an approximating function that attempts to capture important patterns in the data, while leaving out noise or other fine-scale structures/rapid phenomena. Many different algorithms are used in _____. One of the most common algorithms is the 'moving average', often used to try to capture important trends in repeated statistical surveys.
   a. Partial residual plot
   b. Smoothing
   c. 68-95-99.7 rule
   d. Partial regression plot

2. _____ is an adjective for experience-based techniques that help in problem solving, learning and discovery. A _____ method is particularly used to rapidly come to a solution that is hoped to be close to the best possible answer, or 'optimal solution'. _____s are 'rules of thumb', educated guesses, intuitive judgments or simply common sense.
   a. 68-95-99.7 rule
   b. Partition
   c. 8.3 filename
   d. Heuristic

3. A _____ is a principle with broad application that is not intended to be strictly accurate or reliable for every situation. It is an easily learned and easily applied procedure for approximately calculating or recalling some value, or for making some determination. Compare this to heuristic, a similar concept used in mathematical discourse, psychology and computer science, particularly in algorithm design.
   a. 8.3 filename
   b. 68-95-99.7 rule
   c. Back-end database
   d. Rule of thumb

4. _____ is a term used by project managers and project management (PM) organizations to describe methods for analyzing and collectively managing a group of current or proposed projects based on numerous key characteristics. The fundamental objective of the _____ process is to determine the optimal mix and sequencing of proposed projects to best achieve the organization's overall goals - typically expressed in terms of hard economic measures, business strategy goals, or technical strategy goals - while honoring constraints imposed by management or external real-world factors. Typical attributes of projects being analyzed in a _____ process include each project's total expected cost, consumption of scarce resources (human or otherwise) expected timeline and schedule of investment, expected nature, magnitude and timing of benefits to be realized, and relationship or inter-dependencies with other projects in the portfolio.
   a. Project portfolio management
   b. Customer intelligence
   c. Records management
   d. Document Imaging

Chapter 8. Scheduling Resources and Costs

5. _____ is subcontracting a process, such as product design or manufacturing, to a third-party company. The decision to outsource is often made in the interest of lowering cost or making better use of time and energy costs, redirecting or conserving energy directed at the competencies of a particular business, or to make more efficient use of land, labor, capital, (information) technology and resources. _____ became part of the business lexicon during the 1980s.
   a. AACE International
   b. Extreme project management
   c. Outsourcing
   d. AACR2

6. _____ is used to assign the available resources in an economic way. It is part of resource management.

In strategic planning,is a plan for using available resources, for example human resources, especially in the near term, to achieve goals for the future.

   a. Back-end database
   b. Resource allocation
   c. 68-95-99.7 rule
   d. 8.3 filename

7. _____ is an overall management philosophy introduced by Dr. Eliyahu M. Goldratt in his 1984 book titled The Goal, that is geared to help organizations continually achieve their goal. The title comes from the contention that any manageable system is limited in achieving more of its goal by a very small number of constraints, and that there is always at least one constraint. The _____ process seeks to identify the constraint and restructure the rest of the organization around it, through the use of the Five Focusing Steps.
   a. Back-end database
   b. 68-95-99.7 rule
   c. 8.3 filename
   d. Theory of constraints

8. _____ is the discipline of planning, organizing and managing resources to bring about the successful completion of specific project goals and objectives.

A project is a finite endeavor--having specific start and completion dates--undertaken to meet particular goals and objectives, usually to bring about beneficial change or added value. This finite characteristic of projects stands in contrast to processes, or operations--which is repetitive, permanent or semi-permanent functional work to produce products or services.

Chapter 8. Scheduling Resources and Costs

   a. Project management
   b. Risk register
   c. SMART
   d. Logical framework approach

9. The general definition of an _____ is an evaluation of a person, organization, system, process, project or product. _____s are performed to ascertain the validity and reliability of information; also to provide an assessment of a system's internal control. The goal of an _____ is to express an opinion on the person / organization/system (etc) in question, under evaluation based on work done on a test basis.
   a. AACR2
   b. ACID
   c. AACE International
   d. Audit

10. A _____ is a type of bar chart that illustrates a project schedule. _____s illustrate the start and finish dates of the terminal elements and summary elements of a project. Terminal elements and summary elements comprise the work breakdown structure of the project.
   a. 8.3 filename
   b. Gantt chart
   c. Back-end database
   d. 68-95-99.7 rule

Chapter 9. Reducing Project Duration

1. In commerce, _____ is the length of time it takes from a product being conceived until its being available for sale. _____ is important in industries where products are outmoded quickly. A common assumption is that _____ matters most for first-of-a-kind products, but actually the leader often has the luxury of time, while the clock is clearly running for the followers.
   a. Time to market
   b. Service Network
   c. Product life cycle
   d. Sensitivity analysis

2. Models of the _____ effect and the closely related experience curve effect express the relationship between equations for experience and efficiency or between efficiency gains and investment in the effort. The experience of '_____s' was first observed by the 19th Century German psychologist Hermann Ebbinghaus according to the difficulty of memorizing varying numbers of verbal stimuli, and subsequent learning about the complex processes of learning are discussed in the

   The rule used for representing the _____ effect states that the more times a task has been performed, the less time will be required on each subsequent iteration.

   a. 68-95-99.7 rule
   b. 8.3 filename
   c. Back-end database
   d. Learning curve

3. _____ is subcontracting a process, such as product design or manufacturing, to a third-party company. The decision to outsource is often made in the interest of lowering cost or making better use of time and energy costs, redirecting or conserving energy directed at the competencies of a particular business, or to make more efficient use of land, labor, capital, (information) technology and resources. _____ became part of the business lexicon during the 1980s.
   a. AACR2
   b. AACE International
   c. Extreme project management
   d. Outsourcing

4. A _____, sometimes abbreviated to _____, is a type of milestone, benchmark with emphasis on demonstrating progress across all components of a project. It could be considered a project management buzzword, and may have originated in the games industry.

Chapter 9. Reducing Project Duration

a. Technology roadmap
b. Risk register
c. Critical Chain
d. Vertical slice

5. A _____ is an individual or in many cases a business that signs a contract to perform part or all of the obligations of another's contract.

A _____ is hired by a general contractor (or prime contractor) to perform a specific task as part of the overall project. Whilst the most common concept of a _____ is in building works and civil engineering, the range of opportunities for _____ is much wider and it is possible that the greatest number now operate in the information technology and information sectors of business.

a. 68-95-99.7 rule
b. 8.3 filename
c. Legal matter management
d. Subcontractor

6. _____ is the discipline of planning, organizing and managing resources to bring about the successful completion of specific project goals and objectives.

A project is a finite endeavor--having specific start and completion dates--undertaken to meet particular goals and objectives, usually to bring about beneficial change or added value. This finite characteristic of projects stands in contrast to processes, or operations--which is repetitive, permanent or semi-permanent functional work to produce products or services.

a. Risk register
b. Project management
c. SMART
d. Logical framework approach

7. A _____ is a team whose members usually belong to different groups, functions and are assigned to activities for the same project. A team can be divided into sub-teams according to need. Usually _____s are only used for a defined period of time.
a. Project management 2.0
b. Certified project manager
c. Project manager
d. Project team

Chapter 9. Reducing Project Duration

8. _____ is a family of standards for quality management systems. _____ is maintained by ISO, the International Organization for Standardization and is administered by accreditation and certification bodies. The rules are updated, the time and changes in the requirements for quality, motivate change.
   a. ACID
   b. AACR2
   c. AACE International
   d. ISO 9000

9. A _____ is an explicit set of requirements to be satisfied by a material, product, or service. Should a material, product or service fail to meet one or more of the applicable _____s, it may be referred to as being out of specificiation; the abbreviation OOS may also be used.

A technical _____ may be developed privately, for example by a corporation, regulatory body, military, etc.

   a. Back-end database
   b. Specification
   c. 68-95-99.7 rule
   d. 8.3 filename

10. _____s are expenses that change in proportion to the activity of a business. In other words, _____ is the sum of marginal costs. It can also be considered normal costs.
   a. 68-95-99.7 rule
   b. 8.3 filename
   c. Back-end database
   d. Variable cost

11. _____ are costs that are not directly accountable to a particular function or product. _____ may be either fixed or variable. _____ include taxes, administration, personnel and security costs, and are also known as overhead.
   a. Indirect costs
   b. ACID
   c. AACR2
   d. AACE International

12. _____ is a group creativity technique designed to generate a large number of ideas for the solution of a problem. The method was first popularized in the late 1930s by Alex Faickney Osborn in a book called Applied Imagination. Osborn proposed that groups could double their creative output with _____.

a. Item tree analysis
b. Solutions Architect
c. Brainstorming
d. Anthony Judge

Chapter 10. Leadership: Being an Effective Project Manager

1. A _____ is a professional in the field of project management. _____s can have the responsibility of the planning, execution, and closing of any project, typically relating to construction industry, architecture, computer networking, telecommunications or software development.

Many other fields in the production, design and service industries also have _____s.

   a. Project management office
   b. Project manager
   c. Logical framework approach
   d. Schedule chicken

2. In business management, _____ is a management style where a manager closely observes or controls the work of his or her subordinates or employees. _____ is generally used as a negative term.

Webster's Dictionary defines micromanage as: 'to manage with great or excessive control, or attention to details'.

   a. Managing stage boundaries
   b. Micromanagement
   c. Workflow Management Coalition
   d. Mentorship

3. _____ is subcontracting a process, such as product design or manufacturing, to a third-party company. The decision to outsource is often made in the interest of lowering cost or making better use of time and energy costs, redirecting or conserving energy directed at the competencies of a particular business, or to make more efficient use of land, labor, capital, (information) technology and resources. _____ became part of the business lexicon during the 1980s.
   a. Outsourcing
   b. AACR2
   c. AACE International
   d. Extreme project management

4. A _____ is an individual or in many cases a business that signs a contract to perform part or all of the obligations of another's contract.

A _____ is hired by a general contractor (or prime contractor) to perform a specific task as part of the overall project. Whilst the most common concept of a _____ is in building works and civil engineering, the range of opportunities for _____ is much wider and it is possible that the greatest number now operate in the information technology and information sectors of business.

a. 68-95-99.7 rule
b. Legal matter management
c. 8.3 filename
d. Subcontractor

5. _____ indicates a more-or-less equal exchange or substitution of goods or services. English speakers often use the term to mean 'a favour for a favour' and the phrases with almost identical meaning include: 'what for what,' 'give and take,' 'tit for tat', 'this for that', and 'you scratch my back, and I'll scratch yours'.

In legal usage, _____ indicates that an item or a service has been traded in return for something of value, usually when the propriety or equity of the transaction is in question.

a. 68-95-99.7 rule
b. Back-end database
c. 8.3 filename
d. Quid pro quo

6. _____ is a business management strategy aimed at embedding awareness of quality in all organizational processes. _____ has been widely used in manufacturing, education, hospitals, call centers, government, and service industries, as well as NASA space and science programs.

When used together as a phrase, the three words in this expression have the following meanings:

- Total: Involving the entire organization, supply chain, and/or product life cycle
- Quality: With its usual definitions, with all its complexities
- Management: The system of managing with steps like Plan, Organize, Control, Lead, Staff, provisioning and organizing.

As defined by the International Organization for Standardization (ISO):

'_____ is a management approach for an organization, centered on quality, based on the participation of all its members and aiming at long-term success through customer satisfaction, and benefits to all members of the organization and to society.' ISO 8402:1994

One major aim is to reduce variation from every process so that greater consistency of effort is obtained. (Royse, D., Thyer, B., Padgett D., ' Logan T., 2006)

In Japan, _____ comprises four process steps, namely:

1. Kaizen - Focuses on 'Continuous Process Improvement', to make processes visible, repeatable and measurable.
2. Atarimae Hinshitsu - The idea that 'things will work as they are supposed to'.
3. Kansei - Examining the way the user applies the product leads to improvement in the product itself.
4. Miryokuteki Hinshitsu - The idea that 'things should have an aesthetic quality' (for example, a pen will write in a way that is pleasing to the writer.)

_____ requires that the company maintain this quality standard in all aspects of its business. This requires ensuring that things are done right the first time and that defects and waste are eliminated from operations.

a. 8.3 filename
b. 68-95-99.7 rule
c. Back-end database
d. TQM

7. _____ is a business management strategy aimed at embedding awareness of quality in all organizational processes. _____ has been widely used in manufacturing, education, hospitals, call centers, government, and service industries, as well as NASA space and science programs.

When used together as a phrase, the three words in this expression have the following meanings:

- Total: Involving the entire organization, supply chain, and/or product life cycle
- Quality: With its usual definitions, with all its complexities
- Management: The system of managing with steps like Plan, Organize, Control, Lead, Staff, provisioning and organizing.

As defined by the International Organization for Standardization (ISO):

> '_____ is a management approach for an organization, centered on quality, based on the participation of all its members and aiming at long-term success through customer satisfaction, and benefits to all members of the organization and to society.' ISO 8402:1994

One major aim is to reduce variation from every process so that greater consistency of effort is obtained. (Royse, D., Thyer, B., Padgett D., ' Logan T., 2006)

In Japan, _____ comprises four process steps, namely:

1. Kaizen - Focuses on 'Continuous Process Improvement', to make processes visible, repeatable and measurable.
2. Atarimae Hinshitsu - The idea that 'things will work as they are supposed to'.
3. Kansei - Examining the way the user applies the product leads to improvement in the product itself.
4. Miryokuteki Hinshitsu - The idea that 'things should have an aesthetic quality' (for example, a pen will write in a way that is pleasing to the writer.)

_____ requires that the company maintain this quality standard in all aspects of its business. This requires ensuring that things are done right the first time and that defects and waste are eliminated from operations.

a. 68-95-99.7 rule
b. Back-end database
c. 8.3 filename
d. Total quality management

8. Moral psychology is a field of study in both philosophy and psychology. Some use the term 'moral psychology' relatively narrowly to refer to the study of moral development. However, others tend to use the term more broadly to include any topics at the intersection of _____ and psychology (and philosophy of mind.)
  a. AACR2
  b. Ethics
  c. AACE International
  d. ACID

9. _____, first published in 1989, is a self-help book written by Stephen R. Covey. It has sold over 15 million copies in 38 languages since first publication, which was marked by the release of a 15th anniversary edition in 2004. The book lists seven principles that, if established as habits, are supposed to help a person achieve true interdependent effectiveness.
  a. Anthony Judge
  b. The Seven Habits of Highly Effective People
  c. Item tree analysis
  d. Brainstorming

10. _____ , often measured as an _____ Quotient (EQ), is a term that describes the ability, capacity, skill or (in the case of the trait _____ model) a self-perceived ability, to identify, assess, and manage the emotions of one's self, of others, and of groups. Different models have been proposed for the definition of _____ and disagreement exists as to how the term should be used. Despite these disagreements, which are often highly technical, the ability _____ and trait _____ models (but not the mixed models) are enjoying considerable support in the literature and have successful applications in many different domains.

a. AACR2
b. AACE International
c. Emotional intelligence
d. ACID

11. _____ refers to a range of skills, tools, and techniques used to manage time when accomplishing specific tasks, projects and goals. This set encompass a wide scope of activities, and these include planning, allocating, setting goals, delegation, analysis of time spent, monitoring, organizing, scheduling, and prioritizing. Initially _____ referred to just business or work activities, but eventually the term broadened to include personal activities also.

a. Workflow Management Coalition
b. Micromanagement
c. Matrix Management
d. Time management

Chapter 11. Managing Project Teams

1. _____ is the term used to describe a situation where different entities cooperate advantageously for a final outcome. Simply defined, it means that the whole is greater than the sum of the individual parts. Although the whole will be greater than each individual part, this is not the concept of _____.

   a. 8.3 filename
   b. Synergy
   c. Back-end database
   d. 68-95-99.7 rule

2. _____ is a theory in evolutionary biology which states that most sexually reproducing species will experience little evolutionary change for most of their geological history (in an extended state called stasis.) When evolution occurs, it is localized in rare, rapid events of branching speciation (called cladogenesis.) Cladogenesis is simply the process by which species split into two distinct species, rather than one species gradually transforming into another.

   a. 68-95-99.7 rule
   b. Punctuated equilibrium
   c. Back-end database
   d. 8.3 filename

3. _____ is a mental process and is part of the larger problem process that includes problem finding and problem shaping.

   Considered the most complex of all intellectual functions, _____ has been defined as higher-order cognitive process that requires the modulation and control of more routine or fundamental skills. _____ occurs when an organism or an artificial intelligence system needs to move from a given state to a desired goal state.

   a. 8.3 filename
   b. Problem solving
   c. 68-95-99.7 rule
   d. Back-end database

4. A _____ is a professional in the field of project management. _____s can have the responsibility of the planning, execution, and closing of any project, typically relating to construction industry, architecture, computer networking, telecommunications or software development.

   Many other fields in the production, design and service industries also have _____s.

   a. Logical framework approach
   b. Project management office
   c. Schedule chicken
   d. Project manager

Chapter 11. Managing Project Teams

5. _____ is a type of organizational management in which people with similar skills are pooled for work assignments. For example, all engineers may be in one engineering department and report to an engineering manager, but these same engineers may be assigned to different projects and report to a project manager while working on that project. Therefore, each engineer may have to work under several managers to get their job done.
   a. Workflow Management Coalition
   b. Managing stage boundaries
   c. Matrix Management
   d. Micromanagement

6. The _____ is the first meeting with the project team and the client of the project. This meeting would follow definition of the base elements for the project and other project planning activities. This meeting introduces the members of the project team and the client and provides the opportunity to discuss the role of each team member.
   a. Certified project manager
   b. Work package
   c. Business case
   d. Kick-off meeting

7. _____ is the discipline of planning, organizing and managing resources to bring about the successful completion of specific project goals and objectives.

A project is a finite endeavor--having specific start and completion dates--undertaken to meet particular goals and objectives, usually to bring about beneficial change or added value. This finite characteristic of projects stands in contrast to processes, or operations--which is repetitive, permanent or semi-permanent functional work to produce products or services.

   a. SMART
   b. Project management
   c. Risk register
   d. Logical framework approach

8. The _____: KISS is a modern acronym for the empirical principle 'Keep it Short and Simple,' or the more recent and disparaging 'Keep it Simple, Stupid'. KISS states that design simplicity should be a key goal and that unnecessary complexity should be avoided.

The principle most likely finds its origins in similar concepts, such as Occam's razor, and Albert Einstein's maxim that 'everything should be made as simple as possible, but no simpler'.

Chapter 11. Managing Project Teams

a. 68-95-99.7 rule
b. 8.3 filename
c. Back-end database
d. KISS principle

9. _____ in organizations and public policy is both the organizational process of creating and maintaining a plan; and the psychological process of thinking about the activities required to create a desired goal on some scale. As such, it is a fundamental property of intelligent behavior. This thought process is essential to the creation and refinement of a plan, or integration of it with other plans, that is, it combines forecasting of developments with the preparation of scenarios of how to react to them.
a. Planning
b. 68-95-99.7 rule
c. Back-end database
d. 8.3 filename

10. _____ is a project management software program developed and sold by Microsoft which is designed to assist project managers in developing plans, assigning resources to tasks, tracking progress, managing budgets and analyzing workloads.

The application creates critical path schedules, although critical chain and event chain methodology third-party add-ons are available. Schedules can be resource leveled, and chains are visualized in a Gantt chart.

a. 8.3 filename
b. 68-95-99.7 rule
c. RiskyProject
d. Microsoft Project

11. Models of the _____ effect and the closely related experience curve effect express the relationship between equations for experience and efficiency or between efficiency gains and investment in the effort. The experience of '_____s' was first observed by the 19th Century German psychologist Hermann Ebbinghaus according to the difficulty of memorizing varying numbers of verbal stimuli, and subsequent learning about the complex processes of learning are discussed in the

.

The rule used for representing the _____ effect states that the more times a task has been performed, the less time will be required on each subsequent iteration.

a. 68-95-99.7 rule
b. Learning curve
c. Back-end database
d. 8.3 filename

12. _____ is decision making in groups consisting of multiple members/entities. The challenge of group decision is deciding what action a group should take. There are various systems designed to solve this problem.
a. 8.3 filename
b. Nominal group technique
c. Groups decision making
d. 68-95-99.7 rule

13. _____ is a group creativity technique designed to generate a large number of ideas for the solution of a problem. The method was first popularized in the late 1930s by Alex Faickney Osborn in a book called Applied Imagination. Osborn proposed that groups could double their creative output with _____.
a. Solutions Architect
b. Anthony Judge
c. Brainstorming
d. Item tree analysis

14. _____ in the English language is defined firstly as unanimous or general agreement; and secondly group solidarity of belief or sentiment.

Idyllically, achieving _____ requires serious treatment of every group member's considered opinion. Those who wish to take up some action want to hear those who oppose it, because they count on the fact that the ensuing debate will improve the _____.

a. 8.3 filename
b. Back-end database
c. 68-95-99.7 rule
d. Consensus

15. _____, a form of alternative dispute resolution (ADR), is a legal technique for the resolution of disputes outside the courts, wherein the parties to a dispute refer it to one or more persons (the 'arbitrators', 'arbiters' or 'arbitral tribunal'), by whose decision (the 'award') they agree to be bound. It is a settlement technique in which a third party reviews the case and imposes a decision that is legally binding for both sides. Other forms of ADR include mediation (a form of settlement negotiation facilitated by a neutral third party) and non-binding resolution by experts.

a. ACID
b. AACE International
c. AACR2
d. Arbitration

16. _____ is a type of thought exhibited by group members who try to minimize conflict and reach consensus without critically testing, analyzing, and evaluating ideas. Individual creativity, uniqueness, and independent thinking are lost in the pursuit of group cohesiveness, as are the advantages of reasonable balance in choice and thought that might normally be obtained by making decisions as a group. During _____, members of the group avoid promoting viewpoints outside the comfort zone of consensus thinking.
   a. 8.3 filename
   b. Back-end database
   c. 68-95-99.7 rule
   d. Groupthink

17. The _____ is a decision making method for use among groups of many sizes, who want to make their decision quickly, as by a vote, but want everyone's opinions taken into account (as opposed to traditional voting, where only the largest group is considered) . The method of tallying is the difference. First, every member of the group gives their view of the solution, with a short explanation.
   a. 68-95-99.7 rule
   b. Groups decision making
   c. 8.3 filename
   d. Nominal group technique

Chapter 12. Outsourcing: Managing Interorganizational Relations

1. _____ is subcontracting a process, such as product design or manufacturing, to a third-party company. The decision to outsource is often made in the interest of lowering cost or making better use of time and energy costs, redirecting or conserving energy directed at the competencies of a particular business, or to make more efficient use of land, labor, capital, (information) technology and resources. _____ became part of the business lexicon during the 1980s.
    a. AACE International
    b. AACR2
    c. Extreme project management
    d. Outsourcing

2. _____ or contract administration is the management of contracts made with customers, vendors, partners, or employees. _____ includes negotiating the terms and conditions in contracts and ensuring compliance with the terms and conditions, as well as documenting and agreeing any changes that may arise during its implementation or execution. It can be summarized as the process of systematically and efficiently managing contract creating, execution, and analysis for the purpose of maximizing financial and operational performance and minimizing risk.
    a. Government Enterprise Architecture
    b. Federal Enterprise Architecture
    c. Department of Defense Architecture Framework
    d. Contract management

3. _____ is the phenomenon of something getting more intense step by step, for example a quarrel, or, notably, military presence and nuclear armament during the Cold War. (Compare to escalator, a device that lifts something to a higher level.) The term is often said to be originally coined by Herman Kahn in his 1965 work On _____.
    a. ACID
    b. AACE International
    c. Escalation
    d. AACR2

4. _____ is the discipline of planning, organizing and managing resources to bring about the successful completion of specific project goals and objectives.

A project is a finite endeavor--having specific start and completion dates--undertaken to meet particular goals and objectives, usually to bring about beneficial change or added value. This finite characteristic of projects stands in contrast to processes, or operations--which is repetitive, permanent or semi-permanent functional work to produce products or services.

   a. Risk register
   b. Logical framework approach
   c. SMART
   d. Project Management

Chapter 12. Outsourcing: Managing Interorganizational Relations

5. Models of the _____ effect and the closely related experience curve effect express the relationship between equations for experience and efficiency or between efficiency gains and investment in the effort. The experience of '_____s' was first observed by the 19th Century German psychologist Hermann Ebbinghaus according to the difficulty of memorizing varying numbers of verbal stimuli, and subsequent learning about the complex processes of learning are discussed in the

.

The rule used for representing the _____ effect states that the more times a task has been performed, the less time will be required on each subsequent iteration.

   a. 68-95-99.7 rule
   b. Back-end database
   c. 8.3 filename
   d. Learning curve

6. _____ is a systematic method to improve the 'value' of goods or products and services by using an examination of function. Value, as defined, is the ratio of function to cost. Value can therefore be increased by either improving the function or reducing the cost.
   a. 68-95-99.7 rule
   b. 8.3 filename
   c. Back-end database
   d. Value engineering

7. In negotiation theory, the _____ is the course of action that will be taken by a party if the current negotiations fail and an agreement cannot be reached. BATNA is the key focus and the driving force behind a successful negotiator. BATNA should not be confused with the reservation point or walkaway point.
   a. 8.3 filename
   b. 68-95-99.7 rule
   c. Back-end database
   d. Best alternative to a negotiated agreement

8. The _____ is a private, not-for-profit organization whose primary purpose is to develop generally accepted accounting principles (GAAP) within the United States in the public's interest. The Securities and Exchange Commission (SEC) designated the _____ as the organization responsible for setting accounting standards for public companies in the U.S. It was created in 1973, replacing the Committee on Accounting Procedure (CAP) and the Accounting Principles Board (APB) of the American Institute of Certified Public Accountants (AICPA.)

Chapter 12. Outsourcing: Managing Interorganizational Relations

The _____'s mission is 'to establish and improve standards of financial accounting and reporting for the guidance and education of the public, including issuers, auditors, and users of financial information.' To achieve this, _____ has five goals:

- Improve the usefulness of financial reporting by focusing on the primary characteristics of relevance and reliability, and on the qualities of comparability and consistency.
- Keep standards current to reflect changes in methods of doing business and in the economy.
- Consider promptly any significant areas of deficiency in financial reporting that might be improved through standard setting.
- Promote international convergence of accounting standards concurrent with improving the quality of financial reporting.
- Improve common understanding of the nature and purposes of information in financial reports.

The _____ is not a governmental body. The SEC has legal authority to establish financial accounting and reporting standards for publicly held companies under the Securities Exchange Act of 1934.

a. Financial Accounting Standards Board
b. War room
c. PowerLab
d. Social Return on Investment

9. _____, a business term, is a measure of how products and services supplied by a company meet or surpass customer expectation. It is seen as a key performance indicator within business and is part of the four perspectives of a Balanced Scorecard.

In a competitive marketplace where businesses compete for customers, _____ is seen as a key differentiator and increasingly has become a key element of business strategy.

a. Time to market
b. Sensitivity analysis
c. Customer satisfaction
d. Business Technology Management

10. _____, as defined by the _____ Association of America (Information technologyAA), is 'the study, design, development, implementation, support or management of computer-based information systems, particularly software applications and computer hardware.' _____ deals with the use of electronic computers and computer software to convert, store, protect, process, transmit, and securely retrieve information.

Today, the term _____ has ballooned to encompass many aspects of computing and technology, and the term has become very recognizable. The _____ umbrella can be quite large, covering many fields.

a. AACE International
b. Information technology
c. ACID
d. AACR2

11. A _____ is a professional in the field of project management. _____s can have the responsibility of the planning, execution, and closing of any project, typically relating to construction industry, architecture, computer networking, telecommunications or software development.

Many other fields in the production, design and service industries also have _____s.

a. Schedule chicken
b. Logical framework approach
c. Project management office
d. Project manager

12. A _____ is an invitation for suppliers, through a bidding process, to submit a proposal on a specific product or service.

If not stated otherwise, the supplier with the lowest bid is awarded the contract, provided that they meet the minimum criteria for the bid. This is in contrast to a request for proposal (RFP), in which case other reasons (used technology, quality) might cause or allow choice of the second best offer.

a. AACR2
b. Invitation for bid
c. Arrow Diagramming Method
d. AACE International

13. A request for proposal (referred to as _____) is an invitation for suppliers, often through a bidding process, to submit a proposal on a specific commodity or service. A bidding process is one of the best methods for leveraging a company's negotiating ability and purchasing power with suppliers. The _____ process brings structure to the procurement decision and allows the risks and benefits to be identified clearly upfront.
a. RFP
b. Back-end database
c. 68-95-99.7 rule
d. 8.3 filename

Chapter 13. Progress and Performance Measurement and Evaluation

1. _____ is a term used to describe a process of preparing and collecting data - for example as part of a process improvement or similar project. The purpose of _____ is to obtain information to keep on record, to make decisions about important issues, to pass information on to others. Primarily, data is collected to provide information regarding a specific topic .
   a. Public survey
   b. General Social Survey
   c. Test method
   d. Data collection

2. In a general sense, the term _____ refers to a system of people, data records and activities that process the data and information in an organization, and it includes the organization's manual and automated processes. In a narrow sense, the term _____ refers to the specific application software that is used to store data records in a computer system and automates some of the information-processing activities of the organization. Computer-based _____s are in the field of information technology.
   a. AACR2
   b. ACID
   c. AACE International
   d. Information system

3. A _____ is a change implemented to address a weakness identified in a management system. Normally _____s are implemented in response to a customer complaint, abnormal levels of internal nonconformity, nonconformities identified during an internal audit or adverse or unstable trends in product and process monitoring such as would be identified by SPC.

The process of determining a _____ requires identification of actions that can be taken to prevent or mitigate the weakness.

   a. 8.3 filename
   b. Corrective action
   c. 68-95-99.7 rule
   d. Back-end database

4. _____ in project management is the budgeted cost of work that has actually been performed in carrying out a scheduled task during a specific time period. The term is connected with Earned value management and here it is different from:

   - Budgeted Cost of Work Scheduled (BCWS) : the approved budget that has been allocated to complete a scheduled task during a specific time period.
   - Actual Cost of Work Performed (ACWP) : the actual cost that has been spent, rather than the budgeted cost.

As example of the difference assume that a schedule contains:

- a task 'Test hardware' that is budgeted to cost $1000 to perform, and
- is expected to begin at the start of January 1 and
- complete at the end of January 10.

At the end of January 5, the work is scheduled to be 50% complete (5 days of the scheduled 10 days.) So, at the end of January 5,

- the BCWS is $1000 (the budgeted cost) times 50% (the scheduled completion percentage) the work is actually only 30% complete. In this case,

    o the BCWP would be $1000 (budgeted cost) times 30% (the actual completion percentage) suppose that to reach the 30% complete level at the end of January 5, $250 was actually spent.

        ■ Then, the ACWP would be $250.

a. Cone of Uncertainty
b. Student syndrome
c. Mandated Lead Arranger
d. Budgeted cost of work performed

5. A _____ is a type of bar chart that illustrates a project schedule. _____s illustrate the start and finish dates of the terminal elements and summary elements of a project. Terminal elements and summary elements comprise the work breakdown structure of the project.
   a. Back-end database
   b. 68-95-99.7 rule
   c. Gantt chart
   d. 8.3 filename

6. _____ is the discipline of planning, organizing and managing resources to bring about the successful completion of specific project goals and objectives.

A project is a finite endeavor--having specific start and completion dates--undertaken to meet particular goals and objectives, usually to bring about beneficial change or added value. This finite characteristic of projects stands in contrast to processes, or operations--which is repetitive, permanent or semi-permanent functional work to produce products or services.

Chapter 13. Progress and Performance Measurement and Evaluation

a. Project Management
b. Logical framework approach
c. Risk register
d. SMART

7. In probability theory and statistics, the _____ of a random variable, probability distribution averaging the squared deviations of its possible values from the expected value (mean.) Whereas the mean is a way to describe the location of a distribution, the _____ is a way to capture its scale or degree of being spread out. The unit of _____ is the square of the unit of the original variable.
    a. Test set
    b. First-hitting-time models
    c. Standard score
    d. Variance

8. _____s are expenses that change in proportion to the activity of a business. In other words, _____ is the sum of marginal costs. It can also be considered normal costs.
    a. 8.3 filename
    b. Back-end database
    c. 68-95-99.7 rule
    d. Variable cost

9. _____ is the process of estimation in unknown situations. Prediction is a similar, but more general term. Both can refer to estimation of time series, cross-sectional or longitudinal data.
    a. Local convex hull
    b. Power transform
    c. Photoanalysis
    d. Forecasting

10. _____ in project management refers to uncontrolled changes in a project's scope. This phenomenon can occur when the scope of a project is not properly defined, documented, or controlled. It is generally considered a negative occurrence that is to be avoided.
    a. Problem domain analysis
    b. Graphical Evaluation and Review Technique
    c. Scope creep
    d. Student syndrome

11. _____ is the sampling of the real world to generate data that can be manipulated by a computer. Sometimes abbreviated Data acquisitionQ or _____S, Data acquisition typically involves acquisition of signals and waveforms and processing the signals to obtain desired information. The components of _____ systems include appropriate sensors that convert any measurement parameter to an electrical signal, then conditioning the electrical signal which can then be acquired by _____ hardware.
   a. Data acquisition
   b. Test method
   c. Web mining
   d. Two pass verification

Chapter 14. Project Audit and Closure

1. The general definition of an _____ is an evaluation of a person, organization, system, process, project or product. _____s are performed to ascertain the validity and reliability of information; also to provide an assessment of a system's internal control. The goal of an _____ is to express an opinion on the person / organization/system (etc) in question, under evaluation based on work done on a test basis.

   a. ACID
   b. AACR2
   c. AACE International
   d. Audit

2. _____ is a term used to describe a process of preparing and collecting data - for example as part of a process improvement or similar project. The purpose of _____ is to obtain information to keep on record, to make decisions about important issues, to pass information on to others. Primarily, data is collected to provide information regarding a specific topic.

   a. General Social Survey
   b. Test method
   c. Public survey
   d. Data collection

3. A _____ is a professional in the field of project management. _____s can have the responsibility of the planning, execution, and closing of any project, typically relating to construction industry, architecture, computer networking, telecommunications or software development.

   Many other fields in the production, design and service industries also have _____s.

   a. Project management office
   b. Schedule chicken
   c. Logical framework approach
   d. Project manager

Chapter 15. International Projects

1. _____ is the identification, assessment, and prioritization of risks followed by coordinated and economical application of resources to minimize, monitor, and control the probability and/or impact of unfortunate events.. Risks can come from uncertainty in financial markets, project failures, legal liabilities, credit risk, accidents, natural causes and disasters as well as deliberate attacks from an adversary. Several _____ standards have been developed including the Project Management Institute, the National Institute of Science and Technology, actuarial societies, and ISO standards.
   a. Stitch Pipeline
   b. Regression toward the mean
   c. Signals intelligence
   d. Risk management

2. _____ is the identity of a group or culture, or of an individual as far as one is influenced by one's belonging to a group or culture. _____ is similar to and has overlaps with, but is not synonymous with, identity politics.

There are modern questions of culture that are transferred into questions of identity.

   a. Cultural identity
   b. Back-end database
   c. 8.3 filename
   d. 68-95-99.7 rule

3. A _____ in project management and systems engineering, is a tool used to define and group a project's discrete work elements (or tasks) in a way that helps organize and define the total work scope of the project.

A _____ element may be a product, data, a service, or any combination. A _____ also provides the necessary framework for detailed cost estimating and control along with providing guidance for schedule development and control.

   a. 68-95-99.7 rule
   b. Back-end database
   c. 8.3 filename
   d. Work breakdown structure

4. _____ is a term used in subtly different ways in a number of fields, including philosophy, physics, statistics, economics, finance, insurance, psychology, sociology, engineering, and information science. It applies to predictions of future events, to physical measurements already made, or to the unknown.

In his seminal work Risk, _____, and Profit University of Chicago economist Frank Knight (1921) established the important distinction between risk and _____:

   ' _____ must be taken in a sense radically distinct from the familiar notion of risk, from which it has never been properly separated....

a. ACID
b. AACR2
c. Uncertainty
d. AACE International

5. _____ refers to the anxiety and feelings (of surprise, disorientation, uncertainty, confusion, etc.) felt when people have to operate within a different and unknown cultural or social environment, such as a foreign country. It grows out of the difficulties in assimilating the new culture, causing difficulty in knowing what is appropriate and what is not.
   a. Culture shock
   b. Signals intelligence
   c. Risk management
   d. Regression toward the mean

6. The _____ is the phase early in a long-term relationship with a person, place or thing that is characterized by greater than typical joy and lesser than typical friction. Usually during this time there is much more physical contact between the two partners in the relationship. In a political context, it is the early period in a political term during which constituents are less demanding and more forgiving of their representative.
   a. Honeymoon period
   b. 68-95-99.7 rule
   c. 8.3 filename
   d. Back-end database

Chapter 16. Oversight

1. _____ is a term used by project managers and project management (PM) organizations to describe methods for analyzing and collectively managing a group of current or proposed projects based on numerous key characteristics. The fundamental objective of the _____ process is to determine the optimal mix and sequencing of proposed projects to best achieve the organization's overall goals - typically expressed in terms of hard economic measures, business strategy goals, or technical strategy goals - while honoring constraints imposed by management or external real-world factors. Typical attributes of projects being analyzed in a _____ process include each project's total expected cost, consumption of scarce resources (human or otherwise) expected timeline and schedule of investment, expected nature, magnitude and timing of benefits to be realized, and relationship or inter-dependencies with other projects in the portfolio.
   a. Customer intelligence
   b. Records management
   c. Project portfolio management
   d. Document Imaging

2. _____ Programme and Project Management Maturity Model is a reference guide for structured best practice. It breaks down the broad disciplines of portfolio, programme and project management into a hierarchy of Key Process Areas The hierarchical approach enables organisations to assess their current capability and then plot a roadmap for improvement prioritised by those KPAs which will make the biggest impact on performance.
   a. 68-95-99.7 rule
   b. 8.3 filename
   c. Back-end database
   d. P3M3

3. _____ is the discipline of planning, organizing and managing resources to bring about the successful completion of specific project goals and objectives.

   A project is a finite endeavor--having specific start and completion dates--undertaken to meet particular goals and objectives, usually to bring about beneficial change or added value. This finite characteristic of projects stands in contrast to processes, or operations--which is repetitive, permanent or semi-permanent functional work to produce products or services.

   a. Risk register
   b. Logical framework approach
   c. SMART
   d. Project Management

4. Project Management (PM) is a complex and challenging task that strives for solutions and deliverables within time and budget. _____ is an even more daunting task. PM is the discipline of planning, organizing and managing resources to bring about the successful completion of specific project goals and objectives.

Chapter 16. Oversight

a. Virtual project management
b. Scenario planning
c. Micro CMS
d. PHP content management system

5. A _____ is a professional in the field of project management. _____s can have the responsibility of the planning, execution, and closing of any project, typically relating to construction industry, architecture, computer networking, telecommunications or software development.

Many other fields in the production, design and service industries also have _____s.

a. Project manager
b. Schedule chicken
c. Logical framework approach
d. Project management office

6. _____ is a credential offered by the Project Management Institute (PMI.) The credential is obtained by documenting your work experience in project management, completing 35 hours of project management related training, and scoring at least 61% on a written, multiple choice examination. _____ exams administered on or before June 30, 2009 will be based on 'A Guide to the Project Management Body of Knowledge - or PMBOK,' the Third Edition.

a. 68-95-99.7 rule
b. Back-end database
c. 8.3 filename
d. Project Management Professional

7. _____ refers to a developmental relationship in which a more experienced person helps a less experienced person, referred to as a protégé, apprentice, mentoree develop in a specified capacity.

There exists several definitions of mentoring in the literature. Foremost, mentoring involves communication and is relationship based.

a. Matrix Management
b. Workflow Management Coalition
c. Managing stage boundaries
d. Mentorship

ANSWER KEY

Chapter 1
1. a   2. a   3. c   4. d   5. a   6. b   7. b   8. a   9. d   10. d
11. d   12. d   13. d   14. d

Chapter 2
1. c   2. a   3. a   4. c   5. b   6. d   7. d   8. c   9. d   10. b
11. a   12. b   13. d   14. c   15. a

Chapter 3
1. d   2. d   3. b   4. b

Chapter 4
1. d   2. d   3. d   4. d   5. a   6. c   7. a   8. c   9. d   10. d

Chapter 5
1. d   2. b   3. c   4. d   5. b   6. d   7. d   8. c   9. d   10. d
11. c   12. d   13. d

Chapter 6
1. a   2. d   3. d   4. b   5. c   6. b   7. d   8. c

Chapter 7
1. b   2. a   3. a   4. d   5. b   6. b   7. b   8. d   9. c   10. d
11. d   12. d   13. d   14. d

Chapter 8
1. b   2. d   3. d   4. a   5. c   6. b   7. d   8. a   9. d   10. b

Chapter 9
1. a   2. d   3. d   4. d   5. d   6. b   7. d   8. d   9. b   10. d
11. a   12. c

Chapter 10
1. b   2. b   3. a   4. d   5. d   6. d   7. d   8. b   9. b   10. c
11. d

Chapter 11
1. b   2. b   3. b   4. d   5. c   6. d   7. b   8. d   9. a   10. d
11. b   12. c   13. c   14. d   15. d   16. d   17. d

Chapter 12
1. d   2. d   3. c   4. d   5. d   6. d   7. d   8. a   9. c   10. b
11. d   12. b   13. a

ANSWER KEY

Chapter 13
1. d   2. d   3. b   4. d   5. c   6. a   7. d   8. d   9. d   10. c
11. a

Chapter 14
1. d   2. d   3. d

Chapter 15
1. d   2. a   3. d   4. c   5. a   6. a

Chapter 16
1. c   2. d   3. d   4. a   5. a   6. d   7. d